A PAIR OF
LITTLE BEARS

by Alex Behr
illustrations by
Joey Hannaford

Harcourt Brace & Company

Orlando Atlanta Austin Boston San Francisco Chicago Dallas New York Toronto London

Bears live in lairs.

What's in a lair? No
chairs or stairs. Just
bears, bears, bears.

A pair of bear cubs lives in this lair. What a hairy pair of bears!

4

Mother Bear is near the lair. She stays close to her pair of bears.

Mother Bear
thumps into
the lair. She
grunts at her
hairy pair
of bears.

The bears leave their lair
and sniff the air. Bears
know what's there by
sniffing the air.

Mother Bear and
her hairy pair rub
their hair. Bears
have a flair for
rubbing
their hair.

The bears tear at
the bark. The bears look
for grubs there to share.

10

Mother Bear grabs a fish while her hairy pair waits. Mother Bear shows the pair how to fish.

Mother Bear takes care that her little bears don't get hurt. But fishing is a very wet affair!

The bears snort and shake their hair. Bears don't like wet hair.

Pears! Bears like
pears. Mother Bear
and her little bears
share the pears.

13

The bears eat the pears. They get pears in their hair. They toss pears in the air.

Eating pears is a messy affair. But Mother Bear doesn't care. Her little bears are always making messes.

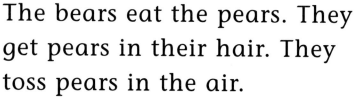

So much fun wears out the little bears. They nap in the pear tree. It has been a good day for the bears.

Animal Information Books
Titles in this Series

Baby Animals
Bears
Birds
Farm Animals
Horses & Ponies
Kittens & Cats

Lions & Tigers
Monkeys & Apes
Puppies & Dogs
Sea Animals
Wild Animals
Zoo Animals

Copyright © 1984 Ottenheimer Publishers, Inc.
Published by Price/Stern/Sloan Publishers, Inc.,
410 North La Cienega Boulevard, Los Angeles, California 90048
All Rights Reserved.
Printed in Brazil.
ISBN: 0-8431-1514-9